Friendship ♥ Gifts from the Heart

Dolley Carlson

illustrated by Beverly Lazor-Banr

FAITHFUL Woman™

For her. For God. For real.
faithfulwoman.com

Little book
be on your way

Bless the reader's
heart I pray

Faithful Woman is an imprint of
Cook Communications ministries, Colorado Springs, CO 80918
Cook Communications, Paris, Ontario
Kingsway Communications, Eastbourne, England

FRIENDSHIP GIFTS FROM THE HEART
© 2001 by Dolley Carlson for text.

Designed by Brenda Franklin
Illustrated by Beverly Lazor-Bahr
Illustration, page 2, by Kathleen O'malley
Edited by Julie Smith

First printing, 2001
Printed in Singapore
1 2 3 4 5 6 7 8 9 10 Printing/Year 05 04 03 02 01

Published in association with Yates & Yates, LLP, Literary Services, Orange, California.

Library of Congress Cataloging-in-Publication Data
Carlson, Dolley.
        Friendship gifts from the heart / Dolley Carlson; illustrated by Beverly Lazor-Bahr
            p   cm.
        ISBN 0-7814-3477-7
        1. Friendship 2. Interpersonal relations. I. Lazor-Bahr, Beverly.
        II. Title.
    BF575.F66 C363   2001
    177'.62--dc21   00-042187

To my friends who are family
and my family who are friends,
Out of the love in your hearts,
mine is fully blessed!

I thank my God every time I remember you.
—Philippians 1:3

Dear friends, let us love one another.
—1 John 4:7

Contents

Introduction

"Be your best friend!" I often heard my daughters and their friends chant to each other as little girls. "Be your best friend if you . . ." The promise of friendship was the most **valuable** thing they had to offer. Every little girl and woman wants a friend and, even better, several friends. How do we make friends? How do we bless those friendships? How do we show we care? How do we forgive when the friendship has gone awry? And what are some wonderful ways to celebrate, cherish, nourish (I've included some favorite recipes), and delight in friendship?

> A friend is a gift you give yourself.
> —Robert Louis Stevenson

The gift of friendship is just that, a gift! When someone lets us into her life we are assured of our ability to connect heart-to-heart and friend-to-friend. Through the ages, stories of great friendships have been recorded in the Bible, literature, music, and even fairy tales. A beloved hymn sings "What a friend we have in Jesus." And it is the presence of Jesus in our hearts that transforms us into vessels of His love pouring gifts from the heart into the hearts of others. Friendship, true friendship, is a gift to be treasured, and it is one of life's sweetest affirmations!

I've written this book for all of us, dear reader, that we may be steadfast in giving tender, loving gifts from the heart to all of our friendships—old, new, and to come. That we may be called friend from across the room, miles, and years.

acceptance
The Gateway to Friendship

Thank heaven for little girls . . .

Self-acceptance is the gateway to accepting and loving others. Poor self-image robs us of blessings and of being a blessing! God had an original pattern just for you, wonderful you! Take out your birth certificate—does anyone else have these very same statistics? Of course not! What's the date on that certificate? That's the day God chose for you to arrive!

Oh you must have been a beautiful baby . . .

God wants us to embrace the wonder of His creation (that would be you) and the depth of His love. Upon hearing "love your neighbor as you love yourself" we often think, it doesn't seem right to love myself. It's okay to love yourself, because you're God's creation! You, with your smile, gifts, and heart. There will never be another you . . . a beautiful and one-of-a-kind pattern, believe it!

You made all the delicate, inner parts of my body and knit me together in my mother's womb.
—Psalm 139:13, NLT

7

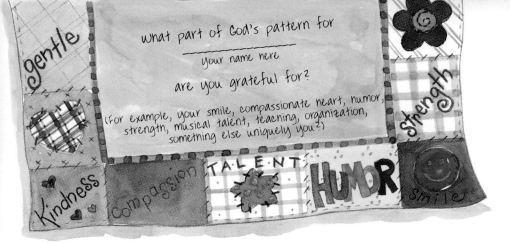

what part of God's pattern for

_____
your name here

are you grateful for?

(For example, your smile, compassionate heart, humor,
strength, musical talent, teaching, organization,
something else uniquely you?)

gentle

Kindness

compassion

TALENT

HUMOR

strength

smile

I know it's not easy to speak of what you appreciate about you . . .
but read Psalm 139:13-15 and keep this precious thought from the Life
Application Bible in mind: "God's character goes into the creation of every
person. When you feel worthless, remember that God's Spirit is ready and
willing to work within you. We should have as much respect for ourselves
as our maker has for us." Amen!

Sometimes . . . a wave of light breaks into our darkness, and it is as though a
voice were saying: "You are accepted."—Paul Johannes Tillich

Sometimes we need the light of Jesus to shine through the heart
of a friend who will call us to **truth**. One woman told me how
a close friend helped her out of the shadows of self-doubt
and into the light of God's love. In honor of their
friendship and the lesson it has for all of us . . .

I'm
Loved Friends

I See the Light!

Of every little nit and nat
That and this . . . . this and that
I had something to say, you see,
Of him or her or you or me!

I used to turn my thoughts this way
For a moment or a day
With second-guessing every action
'Til there was just so much distraction
I missed the boat of peaceful living
And all the fun of friendship giving!

One day a friend came to my door
And said, "This way can be no more.
Both for yourself and those you know
That kind of outlook has to go.
I know you'd love to give and bless
Trust much more and doubt much less.

You're not alone, please know that, friend
We'll talk . . . and pray that this will end.
I've every reason to believe
That from this state you'll be relieved
As you read God's Word of truth and light
Your eyes will see with love-filled sight."

Her words proved true and oh, so wise
For now I see with kinder eyes.
At last, at last I am quite free
To love, to love both you . . .
And me!

God tells us over and over again in the Bible of how much we are loved.
He even calls us "the apple of his eye" (Zechariah 2:8).

9

Acceptance & Little

I have a circle of friends who refuse to let anyone's birthday pass without celebration and affirmation. Talk about acceptance . . . a time is always set aside to affirm the birthday girl! My ears are ringing with dear things these friends have said through the years. "Toni, you're such a good listener." "Anne, your smile is catching." "Patty, your gift of hospitality blesses us all." "Teri, you're always so ready to help . . ."

On and on the gift of acceptance and affirmation goes, each woman appreciating the unique gifts, inclinations, and talents of God's pattern in her dear friend. And we are different! As different as a baking apple is from a sauce apple, alike—'cause they're all apples—but each different in appearance, taste, and purpose. Our friends often have applelike qualities. . . .

Sparkling Cider—This friend smiles, giggles, and exclaims . . . at gatherings, individually, and on the phone too. . . . "Omygoodness, I'm so happy to see you!" She brings the gift of joyous acceptance wherever she goes!

Apple Crisp—She's practical and straightforward . . . crisp, crisp and might say, "We missed you at church on Sunday; were you sick?" Her intent not to embarrass but to let you know you were missed. And if you're missing because of a trial or illness, she'll notice and come immediately to help.

Baked Apple—She may be a bit old-fashioned, but you can always depend on her to be the same, and that's a good thing! No matter what her age, she offers grandmalike wisdom and dependability. Her counsel is delicious!

Gifts of Affirmation

Crab Apple—Has a little comment to make about everything. "Hrumph, I was surprised they had the same menu at the banquet this year as last year—weren't you? What did you think of the speaker?" . . . You need to sweeten this friendship with God's grace and your patience! Eventually she'll respond to His light and your love, honest!

Hot mulled Apple Cider—Just a warm and cozy place to go. A special someone to have a cozy chat with, the kind of friend you can phone anytime—no matter how long it has been since you last talked—'cause she's truly glad to hear from you!

Caramel Apple—This is your sassy friend. She's the one who plans pranks and provides everyone with a good story to take home. She's also the friend who will carry you through a hard time with her joy and attentiveness. She sticks by you no matter what—she's a caramel apple!

You know those birthday celebrations I told you about? Well, Teri's birthday is in October and she never has a cake! That's because I make her a Birthday Apple Crisp every year, candles and all. The "girls" love it, and I hope you and your circle of friends will too.

Happy Birthday Apple Crisp

Let's start at the very beginning . . . .
Preheat oven to 375 degrees

we'll make the topping first . . .

- 1 cup all-purpose flour—no need to sift
- 1/2 cup rolled oats (not the quick-cooking kind)
- 1 cup light-brown sugar, packed
- 1/2 cup butter or margarine, melted

In a large bowl, combine flour, oats, and brown sugar, mix well. Stir in the butter with a fork to make a crumbly mixture. Set aside.

now it's apple time!

- 4 full peeking-over-the-top cups of peeled apples, cut in 1-inch pieces
- 1 cup granulated sugar
- 1/4 cup all-purpose flour—no need to sift
- 1/2 tsp. cinnamon

In another large bowl, combine apples, granulated sugar, flour, cinnamon, and 1/2 cup water. Stir to mix well. Pour into an 8x8x2-inch baking dish sprayed with non-stick spray. Sprinkle topping evenly over filling; bake, uncovered, 35 minutes, or until topping is golden and apples are tender. Serve warm, with ice cream or whipped cream—yummm!

Befriending
If you want a friend . . .

Hello . . . May I call you later?

A man who hath friends must show himself friendly.
—Proverbs 18:24, KGV

Your grandmother said this and so did mine, "Honey, if you want a friend . . . be a friend." People with good friendships make time for friends no matter how busy they are. And we are busy!

Just the other day I phoned my 86-year-old mother-in-law, Marie Carlson, and she was busy! "Oh honey, I can't talk right now. I promised to play the piano at the infirmary, I have a lot of dear friends there. And then my friend Rosy and I are going to lunch and then . . . may I call you later? What's a good time?" She's 86!

Marie's response has many clues for making and keeping friends. Pay attention: this lady received 55 birthday cards last year!

1. Terms of endearment endear! She called me honey! It's fun to have special names—they reveal you are "family" to each other.

2. Serving is a double blessing! Marie promised to play the piano for her dear friends. Many friendships begin and are enriched with a serving heart.

What's a good time?

3. Marie and Rosy made a plan to meet and eat. Getting together for a meal or coffee brings you and your friends to a stopping place where you can talk, relax, and enjoy each other's company with few distractions.

4. "What's a good time to call?" my mother-in-law kindly asked. Her response says, "I really want to talk to you, I just can't right now." Arranging a specific time to phone is practical and sometimes very necessary.

Finders Keepers

Do you find yourself lonely for the company of other women? Why not make a plan for finding new friends and keeping in touch with the old!

make new friends but keep the old
One is silver the other gold.

An Active Idea for Getting Together . . . . How about a running, walking, cycling, or . . . exercise group? You'll be befriending and exercising too! Three times a week my daughter Candy and her friend Cortney take a walk before work. Once Candy over- slept and awakened to an insistent knock on her door. "Cortney, I'm so sorry, please go on with- out me." To which her exercise buddy replied, "Get dressed, Carlson, you're walkin'!"

many a friendship, long, loyal, and self-sacrificing, rested at first on no thicker a foundation than a kind word.
—Frederick W. Faber

Befriending Group Plans

We most often hear this term refer to medical insurance. Well, let's consider this a kind of friendship protection. Hey, we're making a plan! Pastor Joe Aldrich says, "If you aim at nothing you'll hit it every time!"

Once a month—breakfast, lunch, coffee, dinner, investment club, book, gardening, cooking, quilting, memory booking, let's go see a "chick flick," volunteer or special interest, people in your same profession.

Every week or every other week— support group in your special area of need: study, young moms, cancer survivors, health issue, tough love, mourning the loss of a loved one, discipleship, baby-sitting co-op, mentor meeting.

Let's not forget birthdays! You're invited to the **Parties & Celebrations** chapter for more details!

By the way, most of the group plans are suitable for individual plans (you and one friend) as well.

Befriend: To be a friend to; stand by; help in time of need. To become a friend to; make friends with.

15

If we build more windows and fewer walls
we will have more friends."
—Alan McGinnis, The Friendship Factor

Honesty Promotes Friendship

most of us hesitate to be transparent out of
fear of rejection. For years I hid a personal
sorrow, fearful I wouldn't have any friends if I
revealed it . . . . my mother was an alcoholic during my
teen years, and I was never to see the caring mother
of my early childhood again because she died at 37.

Dear reader, I can honestly tell you no one has ever
said, "Dolley, I wanted to be your friend until I heard
your mother was an alcoholic." what they did say was, "so
was mine" or "my father was" or "my brother/sister . . ." and
our hearts met with almost instant affection for having been
through similar trials and heartache. Friendship not founded on
the heartache, but on transparency and understanding.

I become a little more like Jesus
as I follow my God-directed part in "Becoming Real"
one day at a time.—Brenda Waggoner, The Velveteen Woman

A Plan with a Purpose

Praying and being in God's word together grows friendships deep and strong. Consider meeting regularly with several other women to have a Bible study, share your lives, counsel each other, and pray. Rotate the leadership, or invite an older Christian woman to lead you.

When you meet it's essential to keep within a time frame, give everyone a chance to participate, and to be **trustworthy**. what is said must remain confidential. Why not begin praying right now about forming a group and what to study. Long after you stop meeting, heartstrings will bring you together again either in fond memory or happy reunion. I've experienced this, and it is so-so dear.

Give me a few friends who will love me for what I am, or am not, and keep ever burning before my wondering steps the kindly light of hope . . .

People with friends make time for friendship no matter how busy they are. I know four ladies who meet once a week at 6 a.m. Yes, a.m.! They all work but realize the incredible worth of coming together in support and prayer. One woman said, "I was so lonely. It seemed all I did was go to work, clean my house, and grocery shop. I missed my friends but didn't know where I could fit them in. Then Carol came up with the support group idea and life got better, so much better!"

Love wisdom like a sister; make insight a beloved member of your family.—Proverbs 7:4, NLT

Sweets to the Sweet! You Take the Cake(s)!

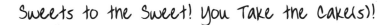

Too little time, tight budget, and need that dessert to travel? A 9x13 cake is the answer! They're easy to prepare, inexpensive, and so portable!

First, frost the cake, score into individual serving sizes but don't cut all the way through until serving time (we don't want a dry cake). Second, decorate for the occasion—whatever it is.

The Gift Cake—"Tied" with real ribbon.

A Floral Cake—Add a small nosegay of fresh flowers.

A Really Happy Cake—Icing hearts, polka dots, or stars, or colored sprinkles, or . . .

Slumber Party Cake—Scoop out enough cake to slip in a little doll, frost the entire cake, outline a pillow, and decorate as the cutest sleeping bag ever.

Feather Your Nest Cake—Angel flake coconut and 3-5 teeny, tiny jelly beans on each square.

Springtime Brownies—Squiggle light green, pink, and yellow ready-made tubes of icing on chocolate-frosted brownies.

"Corny" Chocolate Cake—Pop a candy corn kernel in each square.

Caring
Little Acts Of . . .

The heart benevolent and kind
The most resembles God.—Robert Burns

Caring is love expressed through little acts of kindness, some doing, some speaking, and some just standing alongside. Caring sometimes means we'll have to help our friend over the hard places and troubled waters of life. Will it be easy? Probably not, but we will have walked the way of mercy and kindness for the broken, tired, or grieving heart of a sister-friend. And our bond of friendship will be that much dearer and stronger for it.

Caring also means no gossip! Occasionally out of our need for connectedness we are willing to sell another "sister's" secrets. When a friend has a troubled marriage, rebellious teen, broken heart, financial difficulties, or any situation that makes for juicy gossip she needs our support, confidence, and love.

Joyous caring is being happy for and encouraging our friend's triumphs. Do . . . bake a cake, send a card, give her a bouquet of flowers, balloons, cookies, or praises "in good times and bad times . . . that's what friends are for."

A friend loves at all times.—Proverbs 17:17

Little Acts of . . .

Preparing a Place—Exhausted physically and emotionally, Christi returned home from her mother's memorial service to find a gift from the heart waiting at her front door. Two very close friends, Anne and Suzanne, had prepared for her arrival by freshening the house, changing the bedsheets, putting little vases of flowers here and there, and leaving a beautiful rose on her nightstand. Jesus' presence in the hearts of these two dear friends led them to prepare a place of comfort for Christi's mourning heart.

> God has given us two hands,
> one to receive with and the other to give with.
> —Billy Graham

Simply Showing Up—We sat together in the hospital waiting room and prayed while my husband was in surgery. Later that evening, after taking care of her own family, my friend Teri returned to keep me company during Tom's recovery and the night vigil.

> Let us not become weary in doing good. . . .
> Therefore, as we have opportunity,
> let us do good to all people.
> —Galatians 6:9-10

Tutoring—marlene's son Chep, a bright, much-loved young man, has cerebral palsy. Realizing his determination to go to college and eventually be independent, marlene did everything she could to help her son with his studies. However, she ran into a roadblock when it came to math. It was then that her friend Kathy, a math teacher and the busy mother of three school-age children, stepped forward and committed to tutoring Chep. Well, that was years ago and today Chep's goals have been realized—college, career, and independence!

Baby-sitting—wendy and Larry were twice blessed when they first became parents. The Lord gave them twin boys! Good friends Ted and Diane—young parents themselves—offered to take the babies for a weekend so their parents could have a much-needed time of R & R. Was it easy? NO! Was it a sacrifice? YES! But wendy and Larry will never forget Ted and Diane's gift from the heart; nor will the twins' parents forget how happy their friends looked on returning the babies Sunday afternoon!

Stop, Look, and Listen—These are true-to-life, gifts from the heart stories. The memory of them inspires me to Stop, Look, and Listen for opportunities to give unexpected little acts of care. . . .

Stop, even if it's just for a moment. It's hard to assess needs when you're in constant motion.

Look around: who needs help, encouragement, or a "walking alongside" friend (that's you) bearing a caring gift from the heart?

Listen between the lines for fatigue, hopelessness, overwhelm, or loneliness and then . . .

Go to the Lord in prayer and ask Him to guide your steps and heart in the right direction. Here are a few more caring ideas . . .

a Tisket, a Tasket—If your friend has a loved one in the hospital, bring her a small, simple basket or gift bag of snacks, beverages, and a sandwich. It's often very difficult to leave the patient for even a short while, and although the hospital feeds the patient there's no "room service" for the caretaker.

If your gift is to encourage others, do it—Romans 12:8, NLT

you've Got Mail—Does your friend have a son or daughter away at college, in the armed services, recently married, or relocated, maybe even out of the country? Correspond (snail or e-mail) with her young adult child, and you will have given a caring gift from the heart to both parent and offspring!

We ought to write oftener, if only little notes. The frequency of the expression of affection is a very important thing in human life.—George E. Woodberry

Only a Phone Call Away—Do your friends know you're available for emergency care(ing)? Recently one grateful lady told me how her close friend responded during a crisis. "I was completely devastated and phoned to see if she was by some chance free that afternoon. Her response was a gift in itself: 'I need to make a couple of phone calls and see if I can change some things in my schedule.' One hour later we were sitting on a bench overlooking the ocean and working through my dilemma with advice and prayers."

Winter, spring, summer, or fall,
all you have to do is call, and I'll be there. . . .
You've got a friend.—Carole King

Heart to Heart

Words from my heart, on just a few
I thank the Lord He sent me you
Your friendship and your light-filled way
Bless each and every single day

With ability to hear when I don't tell
You gently say, "Hope all is well"
For times of laughter, joy, and play
And when you ask, "How can I pray?"

As we sit and sip or take a walk
You open the door for one more talk
I love you, sister, and hope to be
The kind of friend you are to me

God bless your heart and bless your way
Until at heaven's gate one day
St. Peter opens heaven's door
And exclaims, "Here comes one more . . .
Angel-friend!"

Dear Emilie's Almond Chicken Tea Sandwiches

Emilie Barnes and tea party are almost synonymous. I am blessed to call her friend and joyous anytime we meet. . . . One sunny afternoon we had a "Tea for Two" lunch in her garden and I'll never forget it! I was in need of counsel, and her sweet smile, wise words, and gentle manner filled my heart to overflowing! Bless you, dear Emilie, bless you.

> 3 boneless, skinless chicken breasts, cooked and
>   chopped coarsely
> 1/2 cup slivered, blanched almonds
> 1/2 cup mayonnaise
> white or wheat bread

Mix chicken, almonds, and mayonnaise. Butter well each slice of bread. On half the slices, spoon about 3 tablespoons of almond-chicken mixture. Top with remaining slices.

Stack three sandwiches tall. Wrap in wax paper and again in a slightly dampened kitchen towel. Let filling set for at least an hour. Unwrap, cut off crusts, and cut into triangles. For a different look, cut sandwiches in 2-inch strips and set on a doily sideways, with the strips of chicken filling showing.

afternoon tea . . .

The mere chink of cups and saucers tunes
the mind to happy repose.
—George Gissing

Tea Party Whimsies

Place a sprig of parsley, a fresh flower,
or even a little trail of ivy on each serving
plate for a touch of whimsy! If there's time . . . a
very narrow ribbon bow on any one of these three is really charming!

For me? Oh, you shouldn't have . . . but I'm so glad you did!

Fill a teacup with dainty candies. Now tip the
on its side allowing the candies to spill onto
the saucer, and a few onto the table too.
You can also do this with sugar cubes if
your tea time dishes don't include a sugar
bowl . . . one lump or two?

Now it's time to . . . place your visit in the hands of the Lord as you
ask His blessing on your conversation, friendship, and tea time.

How delightful is the company of generous people,
who overlook trifles and keep their minds instinctively fixed
on whatever is good and positive in the world about them.
—Van Wyck Brooks

26

The Heart of Friendship-Love!

Give me a few friends who will love me for what I am, or am not,
and keep ever burning before my wondering steps the kindly light of hope.
—Author Unknown

Love truly is the heart of friendship! It's in the giving and receiving of love that friendship is cherished, embraced, protected, and strengthened! How precious and priceless are those three little words . . . I love you. Some wonderful verses in the Bible tell us what love is and is not—their truth a loving standard for all relationships. These heaven-sent truths can be found in 1 Corinthians 13. . . . I call them the "Love Is'es."

Love is patient—when we get to know each other well, there's bound to be a "friendly" characteristic we find annoying—or as my daughters would say, "Really bugs." Draw on the love of the one who dwells within your heart and . . .

Follow His light brightly
Hold faults lightly
Even if you're right(ly)
And say quite politely,
"I'm glad you're my friend!"

Love is kind—Kindness is sometimes defined as "goodness of heart." When your friend excitedly tells everyone about her new discovery, be it a recipe, book, restaurant, . . . and it isn't new to you, let her tell without saying, "I know." Kindly allow her the moment and let goodness of heart be a gift from the heart to your friendship.

What the heart gives away is never gone. . . .
It is kept in the heart of others.
—Robin St. John

It does not envy—Ouch! I know we don't want to be people who envy. But envy can creep up on us during our friend's shining moment of talent, honor, or getting some new thing. Out of its desire to be better, shine brighter, have more, envy can deeply hurt and sometimes break the heart of friendship.

Envy eats nothing but its own heart.—German Proverb

It does not boast—The very minute boasting begins ears grow deaf, feet shuffle, keys jingle, and excuses are made for leaving. Saddest of all, opportunity for friendship often goes out the door as well! There's a difference between telling good, joyous news and boasting. Listen to your heart before speaking one word and ask, "Am I boasting or blessing?"

It is not proud—Pride comes just before the fall, and we don't want to fall out of friendship because of it. Having an attitude of **gratitude** is a sure way to keep out of pride's harmful way.

> To live gratitude is to touch heaven.
> —Johannes A. Gaertner

It is not rude—In friendship do ask questions to get to know each other better, but don't ask questions that are too personal. Do say please and thank you, but don't embarrass with sarcastic humor. And do say, "How may I help?" . . . a lot!

It is not self-seeking—Love is a gift! We're not giving love to get love as in "I love our friendship, now it's your turn." Extend your arms in front of you, palms up, as if you're holding a gift. Now picture your friend receiving the gift. Would you leave your arms and hands in the same position subtly indicating you expect something in return? Of course you wouldn't (I knew that)! So remember, when you're giving words of love they are given to the heart and from the heart as a gift. No expectation, just friendly giving!

29

COUNT TO 10

It is not easily angered—It's tried but true. Count to ten when you feel anger coming on! One, I'm really upset. Two, is it really worth it? Three, please, Lord, help me to keep calm. Four, what's that, Lord? I'm too easily angered? 5-6-7-8-9 . . . 10!

It keeps no record of wrongs—Recalling wrongs keeps every little hurt or slight too fresh. Often we live it all over again! Even worse is the chance that we will share our wrongful memory with someone. When you feel a record-keeping moment coming on be ready to replace that thought with a planned-ahead "this is what I choose to think of instead."

Make that thought a remembered blessing or Bible verse: "Fix your thoughts on what is true and honorable and right. Think about things that are pure and lovely and admirable" (Phil. 4:8, NLT).

Forgive
Forget

Persevere

Love does not delight in evil but rejoices with the truth. It always protects, always trusts, always hopes, always perseveres. Love never fails.
—1 Corinthians 13:6-8

30

I met my friend Rosemary O'Day when we both worked in Boston. At the time I was estranged from God. Week after week Rosemary would invite me (love is kind) to go to church with her, and my answer was always, "no thank you" (love is patient). One day she followed her invitation with four little words that carried me straight into the arms of God: "God's on your side." Our friendship has never waned over time, distance, or absence (love never fails), and I call her my "angel friend" because of her heavenly ways.

when you care Enough to say the very Best . . .

many of my friends and family say "love you" when we part, and sometimes on the answer machine too. "Hi Dolley. Just a reminder to bring a main dish for 12 to the meeting tonight. Love you!" It's easier to hear a message like that when the good-bye is "love you." Dear readers, please don't ever be afraid to express your appreciation, admiration, or love to your friends. . . . Love you!

*Kind words can be short and easy to speak,
but their echoes are truly endless.*
—mother Teresa

31

Boston "Tea Party" Cream Pie

I love the look of this cake with the custard peeking out
between the layers and chocolate frosting drip, dropping down the
sides! First preheat oven according to package directions and get out
all ingredients. Baking pans too!

The Cake

Prepare 1 box of white cake mix according to directions. Bake in two
8-inch cake pans and cool for about 10 minutes. Then remove to wire
racks and cool completely before assembling the "pie."

The Custard

mix Bird's Custard mix (If you can't find custard mix, use one small
box of vanilla pudding—the you-cook-it, not the instant kind.)
according to directions, plus 1/2 tsp. real vanilla. Cool completely before
filling "pie." Same directions for vanilla pudding mix.

The Putting Together

Place one cake layer on a plate, spread custard or pudding over top.
You'll have a little custard left over which can be used for individual
dessert cups. Place second cake layer on top, press down lightly. now
the reason we're even making this cake . . . CHOCOLATE! Delicious . . .

Chocolate Drip-Drop Frosting!

melt 1 square unsweetened chocolate (1 oz.) and 2 tbs. butter on lowest
burner setting and watch closely. Remove from heat. add 1 cup powdered
sugar and 2 tbs. boiling water and beat with electric mixer until
smooth and glossy. Let mixture set for 10 minutes and then
pour over top of "pie" while still warm. The frosting will seem
thin but will thicken in a while. (Refrigerate cake after frosting
has cooled) and, dear baker, you can even put a cherry on top!

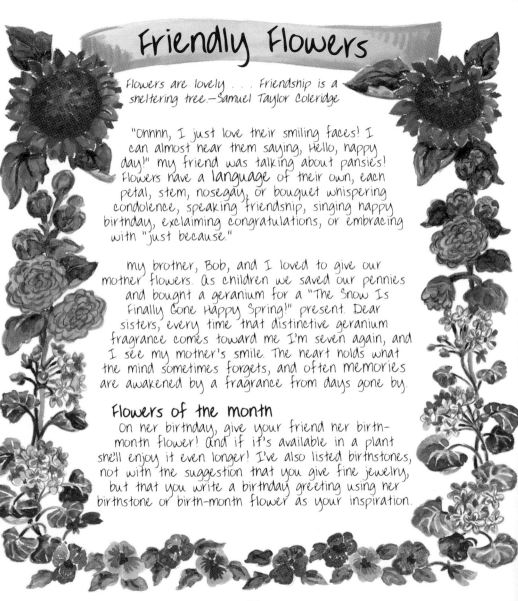

Friendly Flowers

Flowers are lovely . . . Friendship is a sheltering tree.—Samuel Taylor Coleridge

"Ohhhh, I just love their smiling faces! I can almost hear them saying, Hello, happy day!" my friend was talking about pansies! Flowers have a language of their own, each petal, stem, nosegay, or bouquet whispering condolence, speaking friendship, singing happy birthday, exclaiming congratulations, or embracing with "just because."

My brother, Bob, and I loved to give our mother flowers. As children we saved our pennies and bought a geranium for a "The Snow Is Finally Gone Happy Spring!" present. Dear sisters, every time that distinctive geranium fragrance comes toward me I'm seven again, and I see my mother's smile. The heart holds what the mind sometimes forgets, and often memories are awakened by a fragrance from days gone by.

Flowers of the month
On her birthday, give your friend her birth-month flower! And if it's available in a plant she'll enjoy it even longer! I've also listed birthstones, not with the suggestion that you give fine jewelry, but that you write a birthday greeting using her birthstone or birth-month flower as your inspiration.

Happy birthday, _____. How like a violet your friendship is, ever blooming, warm and fuzzy too!

Happy April birthday. They say "diamonds are a girl's best friend," and they're right! Your diamond friendship is the best I've ever known! Happy birthday, friend!

January: Carnation—Fascination (Garnet)
February: Violet—Faithfulness (Amethyst)
March: Jonquil—Affection (Aquamarine)
April: Sweet Peas—Lovely Time (Diamond)
May: Lily of the Valley—Happiness (Emerald)
June: Rose—Love (Pearl)
July: Larkspur—Lightness (Ruby)
August: Gladiolus—Affection (Sardonyx or Perido
September: Aster—Cheerfulness (Sapphire)
October: Calendula—Joy (Opal)
November: Chrysanthemum—Friend (Topaz)
December: Narcissus—Sweet (Turquoise)

Friendship

Hi, 'Lil' Sweet Pea!

This list can be used for your friend's new baby too! I still associate sweet peas with Katie's birth because a close friend brought an armload of them to the hospital on the day she was born. Please don't feel bound by the actual birth-month flower—follow your heart. (Katie's flower is the violet, but sweet peas just suit her.) You could also make a bouquet of the mother and baby's flowers or the whole family's. What a beautiful family!

Flowers for Mom and Dad—Our Very First Friends

When you look up the meaning of flowers and gems for your parents' birthdays, you'll see your parents differently. They'll be happy you took the time to see and blessed by your love and thoughtfulness!

Happy birthday, Dad!

How perfect that your June birthday's flower is the rose and its meaning love. Your love for Mom and all of us has been so selfless. Your love for the Lord has been the foundation and strength of our family.

The Lord bless you and keep you;
the Lord make his face shine upon you
and be gracious to you.—Numbers 6:24-25

Flowers for Baby Dedication

A close friend gave the big sister and the baby teeny, tiny corsages to wear at the baby's Sunday morning dedication. Divine intervention must have kept that corsage on the baby—she never pulled it off. Today it is pressed in her baby book, a reminder of friendship, thoughtfulness, and even better, the recognized importance of that holy event.

The good man brings good things
out of the good stored up in his heart.
—Luke 6:45

'Til we meet again . . .

Shirley had gone home to heaven after a long battle with cancer. Her husband made a unique request for her memorial service. "Please only bring flowers from your garden." Words can't do justice to the vision of hundreds of homemade bouquets brought in honor of a gentle woman whose sweet fragrance of love and mercy had gently wafted its way into the hearts of so many.

Good-bye & God Bless You

We were leaving Ukraine after eight days of teaching, learning, eating, and singing. Our hearts overflowed with love and appreciation for our new friends. While going through customs we heard Oksana's voice above all the din, "Carol, Dolley, wait . . . I have brought to you the first flower of spring; you must have it for your journey. I love you, God bless you!" Her gift of edelweiss—"blossom of snow, may you bloom and grow forever"—and her gift from the heart will bloom in our hearts forever. Bring flowers for friends' coming and going. Practical? No, but filled with love and blessing!

> may the Lord keep watch between you and me
> when we are away from each other.
> —Genesis 31:49

36

Forgiveness

The most Expensive Gift of all

Humility

If you hold anything against anyone,
forgive him—Mark 11:25

How in the world did we get here?
you may ask when in conflict with a
friend. How did this happen? Will I
forgive . . . or not? Forgiveness is
the most expensive gift of all! Its
price: giving up anger, hurt, or humbly sacrificing the need
to be right. The love and wisdom of one particular entry
in *Life's Little Instruction Book* touched my heart: "Never
cut what can be untied." It's a cinch to cut and run!
Anyone can do that. Though painful for the moment, great blessings
come from working out the knots and taking the high road.

Sorrow

Jesus forgives us and asks us to forgive each other "seventy times seven"
times. But Satan will always try to break what Jesus has made whole and
says, "Don't do it! Don't forgive! Remember! Remember!" When your conflict plays over and over in your mind, the point of no return is right
around the corner.

If a relationship has soured,
examine yourself, not the other,
take the humble stance, confess and ask to be forgiven.
In each case, you'll break through to God's renewal.
—Ray and Anne Ortlund

Hope

The road to forgiveness is not an easy one in asking or giving. Yet most friendships find themselves in need of the trip sooner or later, with emotions meeting at the crossroads of Prideful Way or the Peaceful Route. Does your heart need directions? It's easy to get lost in disappointment and drive around in circles of anger or hurt feelings. I've been on the road to forgiveness; just take a right turn at Love (you'll see Compassion on the way), gently yield to Humility, and before long you'll find Forgiveness on your right side.

Lay down the burden of your heart,
I know you'll never miss it.
—Jesse Winchester

"Dear friends, let us love one another . . ." Not long ago I was struggling with a friendship and thought, Boy, is she a piece of work. I heard the Lord agree with me, "Yes she is! She's my piece of work, and she needs your love." Talk about an attitude change. It helps so much when emotions are running high to remember that our friend is beloved by God.

Forgiveness is the ultimate triumph of good over evil.

Be kind to each other, tenderhearted,
forgiving one another,
just as God through Christ has forgiven you.
—Ephesians 4:32, NLT

Friendship-Breaking, Conflict-making mistakes!

Gossip
"Troublemakers start fights; gossips break up friendships" (Prov. 16:28, TM).

Jealousy
"We're blasted by anger . . . but who can survive jealousy?" (Prov. 27:4, TM).

Petty Differences
"Be easy on people; you'll find life a lot easier" (Luke 6:37, TM).

Comparison
"You're blessed when you're content with just who you are—no more, no less" (Matt. 5:5, TM).

So many conflicts begin with what we say. "Out of the overflow of the heart the mouth speaks" (Matt. 12:34). A love-filled heart speaks and lives loving friendship. We need to fill our hearts with God's truth so there'll be no room for Satan's lies! God's truth, yesterday, today, and forever . . . true!

What Are Your Emotions Saying? Look up your emotion in a Bible concordance. For example, Proverbs 15:1 talks about anger: "A gentle answer turns away wrath, but a harsh word stirs up anger." Learn from God's Word and gently say, "I'm sorry this tension has developed between us. Please help me to understand how it happened, and I'll do my very best to resolve our differences." A gentle answer strongly says, "You mean more to me than getting the last word!"

If you know someone well enough to be in conflict, you know her well enough to pray for her needs. Prayer really is the ONLY way we can prepare our hearts and bruised feelings to move toward forgiveness.

When we choose not to forgive, it's like letting the other person live in our head rent free—Lee Ezell

On Bended Knee—Kneeling brings us to a reverent and centered time of prayer. However, please know God hears our prayers no matter our posture, location, clarity, or volume. He hears us because He loves us, and He's always listening for the voice of His beloved child . . . that's you!

Years ago I began saying a little prayer before speaking engagements: "Take me out, Jesus, and put You in." That prayer has since spilled over into every area of my life. Emptying our hearts of self makes more room for His gifts of love and grace and mercy—love and grace and mercy to forgive and forgive and forgive. . . .

Lord, please let my words be tender and sweet because someday I may need to eat them.

Ouch, That Hurts!

Do you ever find yourself saying, "You're too sensitive." Chances are something has bumped up against an old wound. Saying "I'm sorry" when it seems unmerited is a grace-filled gift from the heart. And for those of you who are "too sensitive," forgiveness is the golden thread that mends a broken heart. So please ask God to help you to take the first step toward forg

> To forgive means to write it off. Let it go.
> Tear up the account. It is to render the account "canceled."
> —Dr. Henry Cloud & Dr. John Townsend, Boundaries

Time Out

I've learned that when feelings are hurt or deep disappointment comes our way the best thing to do is . . . hesitate . . . for however long it takes to get a more rational perspective on the situation. (But please don't confuse hesitation with "the silent treatment.") Maybe you are overreacting. Try not to be impulsive, and give yourself some time to—as the Supremes sing—"think it o-o-ver." However, if the situation needs to be addressed on the spot you could say, "How about discussing this later in the week?" or "In all honesty, I need a few minutes, hours, days . . . to think and pray." Then, dear reader, do it: think and pray. Grandma says, "You can't take back words; they stick, so we need to choose our words very carefully."

Five Ways to Ask Forgiveness

Please forgive me? (That's original!)
I made a terrible mistake when . . .
There's no excuse for what I did . . .
I don't know what I was thinking when . . .
I'm very competitive, that's where the trouble began . . .

Dear readers, it's essential to state what the offense was, not bemoaning the fact but clarifying it: I don't know what I was thinking when I spoke to you that way. Please forgive me?

Five Ways to Give Forgiveness & Be Happy About It

I forgive you. (Originality once again!)
It just didn't seem like you to . . .
I know you've been under a lot of stress . . .
Please know that I really want our friendship to survive this . . .
I don't think you really meant to hurt me . . .

And once again, clarifying will prevent future misunderstanding: It just didn't seem like you to repeat the secret I told you. I forgive you.

> If a fellow believer hurts you, go and tell him—
> work it out between the two of you.
> If he listens, you've made a friend.
> —Matthew 18:15, TM

42

Prayer
Heartfelt & Specific
Ways to Pray

I always thank my God as I remember you in my prayers.—Philemon 4

It's such a comfort to know someone is praying for you. Whatever our age or stage we all need prayer. Prayers give us **immediate** access to God. No appointment to be made, calendar to be checked, schedules to be coordinated. He's always there, waiting for our conversation with Him, one-by-one, two-by-two, or grouped . . . in prayer.

And on how prayer enriches our friendships. Through requests for prayer friends learn of each other's needs, a pledge to pray assures us of devoted friendship, and answered prayers bring our hearts **together** in praise and thanksgiving!

Flower Power
We were having brunch in Linda's home when another friend asked us to pray for her son, recently admitted to a rehab center. Just then a tiny daisy fell from the centerpiece, and I saw it as a perfect prayer reminder. At home I placed it on a shelf I see every day. All the ladies in our group prayed diligently, and today that boy is in a healthy, productive lifestyle. He has a very happy mom!

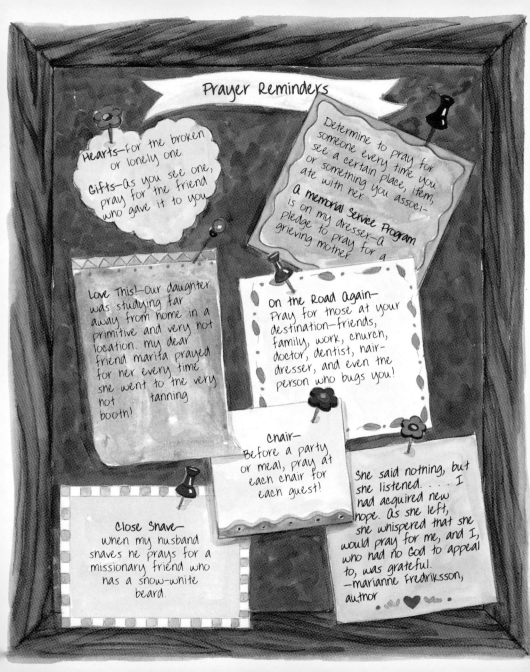

Prayer Reminders

Hearts—for the broken or lonely one.

Gifts—As you see one, pray for the friend who gave it to you.

Determine to pray for someone every time you see a certain place, item, or something you associate with her.

A memorial Service Program is on my dresser—a pledge to pray for a grieving mother.

Love This!—Our daughter was studying far away from home in a primitive and very hot location. my dear friend marita prayed for her every time she went to the very hot . . . . tanning booth!

On the Road Again—Pray for those at your destination—friends, family, work, church, doctor, dentist, hairdresser, and even the person who bugs you!

Chair—Before a party or meal, pray at each chair for each guest!

Close Shave—When my husband shaves he prays for a missionary friend who has a snow-white beard.

She said nothing, but she listened. . . . I had acquired new hope. As she left, she whispered that she would pray for me, and I, who had no God to appeal to, was grateful.
—marianne Fredriksson, author

A Gift from the Heart and for the Heart

By praying not only does your heart give a precious gift, it receives one as well . . . the gift of time . . . with your Heavenly Father!

Ruth Bell Graham uses a phrase that is so helpful: "in the way of your life." We can apply this practical advice to praying. For example, Lois is a grandmother who prays for countless family and friends at very specific times throughout the day "in the way of her life." Just last Sunday a concerned mother said to me with great hope, "Lois prays for my daughter every day on her morning walk."

> He walks with me,
> and He talks with me,
> and He tells me I am His own.

Good morning, Lord!

Pray before even leaving your bed. Pray very specifically from head to toe. For instance, "Lord, please bless the direction my feet take, and let me be a blessing when I get there." Then heart, hands, eyes, mouth, ears, mind . . . for protection, guidance, and God's holy blessing on the day. You can also pray this way for your close friend, mother, sister, teenager . . . those whose needs you know really well.

> O God,
> . . . early will I seek thee.
> —Psalm 63:1, KJV

45

Rest and be thankful.—William Wordsworth

Good night, Lord!

Reading a few verses from the Bible and saying a little prayer just before we tuck in is what my mother-in-law calls "an anointing on the next day." A friend told me about a gift from the heart she gave to her entire family and friends too—a copy of the same devotional, each page specifically dated. "We live far apart and my sister is in Australia so I thought this would be a good way for everyone to remember each other because we'd all be on the same page!"

I like what Cliff Barrows says about prayer: "Isn't it a relief to discover that getting your sentences to come out right isn't what prayer is about! Rather, prayer is simple, ongoing conversation with our Heavenly Father that is honest and heartfelt. How exciting it is when we begin to discover that, through prayer, His goodness and power are changing lives—ours and those we've been praying for."

Yes and Amen!

Friends Who Pray Together Stay Together

Join as prayer partners for each other's children or grandchildren. Through the years, we've prayed for Gail and Peter's four daughters, and they for our two. Each prayer request is very specific, and we communicate primarily by phone. "We have six girls to pray for" is what we've always said, and now we have nine girls! They're grandparents!

Ka Ka Ka Katies!

Katie C., Katie Y., and Katie P.—"The Katies"—is how Susan, Julie, and I refer to the girls when we each ask prayer for their young lives. All three are students (one just graduated—yea!). And I just love hearing all the "Katie did" stories, like what Katie Y. did this last Christmas. She secretly collected her mother's recipes, made crisp new copies, and housed them in a really cute box. "Where is that recipe now?" Susan asked while frantically searching for her favorite tortilla soup. Katie kept her secret until Christmas morning. When Susan opened the gift . . . joy and joy again at the thought of Katie's love and her perfect gift from the heart!

Tortilla "where is that recipe now?" Soup

First, get out all the ingredients including your food processor or cutting board.

6 cups chicken broth
1 1/2 cups chopped leeks
3 stalks celery, chopped.
2 14-oz. cans Mexican stewed tomatoes
8 oz. tomato sauce
Generous 1/2 tsp cumin
Salt and pepper to taste
1 yellow squash (crookneck) and
2 zucchini, cut bite size
3 carrots, diced
1 clove garlic, minced
1 c. frozen corn
6-8 chicken thighs, cooked and shredded
1/2 c. fresh cilantro
Sour cream (optional)

Combine all ingredients except cilantro and sour cream. Bring to a boil, then reduce heat and simmer 45 to 60 minutes. Add cilantro (chopped) for the last 20 minutes. A little dollop of sour cream sprinkled with finely chopped cilantro is the perfect topping! And be sure to have a bowl of fresh salsa on the table for those who want their soup a little *picante*—hotter! Serve with a basket of warm tortillas, cornbread fresh from the oven, and lots of butter. *mas delicioso!*

Everything Is Relative!
Mothers, Daughters, Sisters, & In-Laws, too!

Every woman wants a "sister-friend." Those two words together say it all! Many of us have sister-friends and mother-friends within our families. These friendships are the easiest to take for granted because they've always been there. And you may have the blessing of adding even more women to your family circle of friends through in-law relationships. Our immediate and in-law family relationships have the potential to be cliché or cherished, broken or blessed, endured or enjoyed. When sister-friends are true-to-life family, we are twice blessed with kinship and friendship!

Blest be the tie that binds our hearts in Christian love.

Prayer Chain—Links of Love
Prayer creates a strong link between friends, and when our sister-friends (or daughter-friends) feel free to ask for prayer it creates a precious gift from the heart "prayer chain" between us. My husband's sister, Connie, and I frequently phone each other asking for or reporting answers to prayer. When my phone (or hers) rings in the early morning it's almost always the sister calling: "Oh, I'm glad you're home. . . . Would you please pray for . . . thanks. Love you!"

The strongest sibling bond (and the highest phone bills) is . . . between sisters.
—Dee Brestin, We Are Sisters

49

Once her child marries, a woman sometimes finds herself regarded as a cliché with the title mother-in-law! When families come together there are bound to be differences, but they don't need to become monumental. I imagine Naomi of the Bible wasn't too thrilled when her boys married Moabite girls. "Elimelech, she only cooks Moab. I hope our son is getting enough to eat, and have you noticed her tent keeping?" Oh what a blessing young Ruth became. In Naomi's darkest hour, Ruth's loyalty lit the way home to Bethlehem.

A young woman needs all the affirmation she can get as she establishes her marriage and home.

Mothers of sons, this is the woman he loves. The best wedding gift you can give him is to love her. One groom asked, "Do you like her, mother?" And his mother replied, "Of course I do. She's your joy, so she's my joy too."

And mothers of daughters, we need to help our daughter "leave and cleave." Encouraging her to be a wife first and daughter second will put you in first place with your son-in-law!

Be Loyal... Love Her... Affirm... Encourage...

Let's Play Dress Up!

Little girls just love to play dress up!
I can almost hear the sound of
little feet in oversized high heels—
scrape, clunk, scrape, clunk—and
the memory of my own little girls saying, "Look at me, mommy. I'm just like you!"

Teens shudder at the thought of being just like mom, but only a few years later they'll seek your wisdom and embrace your kinship. Mothers of teens . . . this really happens! As the mother of two young adult daughters, I can tell you that when all is said and done these girls are my closest friends, my forever friends, and that's what we want . . . not only kinship, but friendship too. Here's a checklist for mothers of daughters. I hope you'll feel twice blessed 'cause I have two entries for each letter of . . .

DAUGHTER

Delight in her and speak of your delight, every chance you get!
Don't compare her to others, correct her in public, or tell her business to anyone.

I'm so proud of you!

Assume the best!
Ask how she's doing even if you know the answer will be, "Fine, can I go now?"

Understand by remembering how you felt at her age, whether she's 6, 16, or 36! Put yourself in her shoes. **U**nappreciated is what you'll sometimes be. Just wait; your day will come, honest!

Give her your love every day. Love she can hear: "I love you," love she can see: little notes; love she can feel: hugs. One mother said of hugs, "I never let go first!" She made this decision after hugging her teenager and waiting for her to let go. . . . She didn't for a long time and the mother was stunned. "So now I never let go first!" Hugs speak volumes of "I love you." Get counsel from a family member, your pastor, or a professional counselor if a situation has gone beyond your grasp. There is no stigma to seeking professional counseling. God sends us helpers.

Hats off to her accomplishment . . . even if it's just washing the dog!
Hold on to God's promise of giving "hope and a future" to His children.

teach her by example—I know, eeeeek! But mom, that's how she'll learn best.
Tickle her fancy: lunch out, a movie, a slumber party at your house, whatever her joy is!

XXOO

enjoy her! Look for the joy . . . even in the hard places. This is my daughter, my forever friend, my dear!
Encourage her toward Jesus when she's young and in Jesus when she's older.

Regard her always with respect no matter the age or stage of her life.
Remember she's your little girl, and there will never be another one like her, a gift from God's heart to yours.

Don't talk to your adult children about Jesus, talk to Jesus about your adult children.—Margaret Jensen, author & speaker

most of what's said in *Daughter* can be applied to all of our relative relationships, whether mother, sister, cousin, aunt, grandmother, or in-law. Okay, let's talk about in-laws . . . .

Daughter-in-Law, Sister-in-Law

Your mother-in-law is the mother of the man you fell in love with. Why not write her a gift from the heart letter thanking her for raising such a wonderful son? And please know that one of the best gifts you can bring to your marriage is love for your husband's family. "Your people will be my people" (Ruth 1:16). My husband's sister, Connie, never introduces me as her sister-in-law; she always says, "This is my sister, Dolley."

Sisters, sisters, there were never such devoted sisters.
—1950s pop tune

For Motherless Daughters

Dear ones, please know Jesus is near to the brokenhearted, and He meets us where we are, sobbing, depressed, angry, or simply lonely. Sometimes that meeting comes from the heart of a listening friend (maybe you're the friend) or an older relative (maybe you're the older relative) with stories to tell of days gone by. My Aunt Jane does this, and I can't begin to say how much it means to me. And to you the daughter, if you feel the need to cry, please cry. Our hearts and souls need to process and mourn loss, and tears thankfully soften immediate grief and eventually contribute to our overall sense of peaceful closure.

I still hold tight. She lives on beneath everything I do. . . . Loss is our legacy. Insight is our gift. memory is our guide.
—Hope Edelman, motherless Daughters

a "Relative" Gift from the Heart

Several years ago my mother- and father-in-law gave me a gift from the heart that still brings tears to my eyes. By the time I was 23 both of my parents were deceased and my husband's mother and father were the only parents my adult life would hold. I was feeling a little displaced and told my mother-in-law of my sadness.

memorial Day was only a week away, and shortly after the holiday I received this note from her: "We got up early, drove to the cemetery [where my parents are buried], and had a short, sweet, one-sided conversation. 'we never got to know you folks, but we want to thank you for your daughter. She has made our son a wonderful wife, and she is a wonderful mother to our two lovely granddaughters. She is our daughter now, and we love her very much.' Then we placed two red roses in a vase by the american flag in front of the stone. With much love, marie and Dave."

A Token of My Love

Giving presents to each other symbolizes much more than a gift in the hand. It represents a place in your heart. When in-laws, especially mothers-in-law, give anything that has been in the family for a while it really says, "I expect you'll be with us forever!" When mothers give to daughters, and daughters to mothers, or any combination of relative gift exchange takes place, it sweetly says, "I wanted to please you because I love you and we're family!"

The future mother-in-law:

"My father gave this pin to my mother when they first fell in love. I wanted you to have it." The bride, moments before walking down the aisle: "Oh thank you, I needed 'something old.' It's beautiful." Dolley . . . and Marie Carlson

> I love that we're a Family

Dear Sister-Friends,

Throw caution to the wind. Tell your relatives you love them a lot and you're happy as can be that you're FAMILY! Then hug them and don't let go first! God bless you and yours!

We also pray that you will be strengthened with his glorious power.
—Colossians 1:11, NLT

56

Parties & Celebrations

Honor, Love, Laughter, & Joy!

How shall we celebrate? There are parties big, small, elaborate, and simple, but no matter the reason everybody loves to be on the guest list! The very invitation is a gift from the heart that says . . . you are a valued friend and without you it just wouldn't be the same!

> The Honor of Your Presence Is Requested
> You're Invited To
> Please Join Us
> Y'all Come Now!

Make your home speak PARTY! before the guests even cross the threshold. Helium balloons or flowers tied with streams of ribbons to the mailbox or a banner by your front door announces, "We were expecting you, welcome!"

Parties, Parties, Parties

So cute!

Recently at a baby shower, folded diapers (new, of course) were our luncheon napkins! As the expectant mother opened each gift, the giver shared a little motherly advice or story, all gifts from the heart to everyone present!

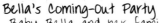

Bella's Coming-Out Party

Baby Bella and her family live in another state, but when she came to visit, Grandma had a "Please Come meet the new Baby" tea party. This was a gift from the heart for mom Kristi, too, as she joyously introduced her baby daughter to old friends!

A Gentle Shower of Grace and Love

Is what the ladies' Bible study gave for my friend's daughter, an unwed mother. A new life was coming into the world, and what could have been a time of ignoring the obvious became a baby gift from the heart to a young girl who needed not only practical gifts but the greatest gift of all . . . love!

Little After-School Parties

Are what we called our three o'clock time together. My girls would always come home from school hungry, and our routine was to have a "party" with something to eat and visit. That little ritual created a heart path that is traveled to this day.

Don't miss the joy of Great-Grandmas

Spend some time with one of these "greats"—yours or someone else's—and you'll be greater for it! Why not have a "greatest generation that ever lived" party or tea party? These dear women are going home to heaven by the thousands. Don't miss the opportunity to have a great celebration!

A Bevy of Birthday Party Ideas

Please Wear All White

Is what the invitation said for Joanne's birthday party. It was outdoors and very romantic. Asking guests to all wear the same color or type of clothing adds a festive touch to any party!

Honor Your Heritage

Patty's friends chose to honor her Native American roots and decorated with family artifacts. Omaha is her tribe and generosity is her heart. I wrote a poem personalized to my Indian princess friend. "By the shores of Big Corona, in the village . . ."

When Your Friend Isn't Feeling So Young

How about a "little girl" party? Friends did this for my fortieth birthday, and it was hilarious—everyone dressed as little girls! It was to be a surprise for me, but I had one for them. . . . I came as Peter Pan!

Secretly Gather Pictures

Of your friend at different times in her life, and use them as part of the decorations. Your invitation could say, "Picture This . . ." and on the inside a vintage picture of the guest of honor. Ask each guest to share a "picture" she has in her heart of the birthday girl; maybe how they met or "I knew I wanted to be friends when—" Each "snapshot" a gift from the heart that will keep forever.

True to my Irish heritage, one of my favorite celebrations is a

St. Patrick's Day Dinner
Corned Beef & Cabbage & . . .Those Potatoes!

    4-5 lb. corned beef brisket
    1 medium clove garlic
    1 medium yellow onion, halved
    2 whole cloves
    10 whole black peppercorns
    2 bay leaves
    2 1/4 tsp mustard seed
    (Or substitute the seasoning packet that comes
    with the beef.)
    1 medium head of cabbage, cut into wedges

Rinse corned beef quickly under cold water and place in large pot; cover with cold water. Add remaining ingredients, except cabbage. Bring to boil. Lower heat, simmer for 5 minutes. As foam forms on the water, skim it off with a spoon. Cover, lid slightly askew; simmer 3 to 4 hours, or until fork-tender. Add cabbage last 15 minutes.

To serve: Remove corned beef and cabbage from liquid. Drain cabbage. Slice corned beef; arrange on platter with parsley garnish. Place cabbage wedges in a covered bowl so they stay hot! mmmmmmmmm!

Boiled Potatoes with Parsley Butter

    2 dozen or more small red potatoes
    1 bunch of fresh parsley and butter (the real thing)

Gently scrub potatoes. Peel a little strip from the middle of each. Place in a large pot and cover with cold water. Heat until boiling, reduce heat, and simmer until tender, about 20-25 minutes. When cooked, gently strain off water. When the potatoes are almost ready melt butter. (You decide how much—we almost drown our potatoes!) Add chopped parsley and pour over potatoes.

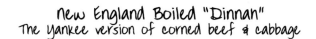

new England Boiled "Dinnah"
The yankee version of corned beef & cabbage

add 6 each medium carrots, white turnips or parsnips, and potatoes, pared and cut in fourths, to corned beef and cabbage during last 25 minutes of cooking.

with both dinners serve assorted mustards and horseradish.

Irish soda bread makes a perfect accompaniment, and shamrocks a perfect centerpiece. I buy two small pots, place them in baskets, and let them "march" down the table between candles. It's an Irish blessing to send your friends home with a "little something." maybe a small loaf of soda bread wrapped in cellophane and tied with green ribbon, or "Please take home one of the shamrocks."

Did you know? St. Patrick used the shamrock to explain the Holy Trinity to all of Ireland: three but one—Father, Son, and Holy Spirit.

an Irish Blessing

may the sunshine always brighten your heart
and your cares be gone with the morrow
may the hand of a friend always be near
In good times and in those of sorrow
may our Heavenly Father hold and keep you
Safe in the palm of His hand
may our homes, my friend, be next to each other
when we reach Eternity's land.

My House

Location, Location

Let Them Eat Cake

Some extra touches make a favorite restaurant a little more special. Bring a centerpiece—a few flowers in a small vase are charming—and have a party favor at each place. Add pretty paper napkins, place cards, and your party is ready to go! Be sure to let the restaurant know you'll be bringing a birthday cake.

Park

Brown Bag Birthday Picnic

Have everyone pack a brown bag lunch and explain that it will be in a basket of surprise lunches. This creates happy camaraderie among guests: "Who brought this delicious sandwich? Amy, was that you?" Bring a blanket, meet at a park, and have each guest contribute to the party making with a centerpiece, dessert, beverage, or even music (portable tape or CD player). Joy!

Cafe

Celebrating Life & Friendship!
Sister Act

Living too far away from each other to make frequent visits, Karen and her sisters met only at family events. And that just wasn't enough. So now they meet once a month at a central location for dinner and a movie. "I look at these women and realize how blessed I am. They're my real honest-to-goodness sisters!"

Shopping

Lake

Theater

Your House

We're Getting Together at my House

The Lord put it on mary's heart to host a monthly
meeting for all the "girlfriends." when our children
were little we saw each other often, but now
don't see each other nearly enough. It's in the
evening, snacks and desserts are served (different
people bring them each month), and there's a
specific question to keep our discussion directed.
Omygoodness, the blessing of being together
again! Is it a late night? absolutely, but so
worth it!

Beach

Celebration & Party Bouquet

Have each guest bring a flower—silk or
fresh—for the honored friend and tell why it
reminds them of her. maybe nasturtiums
because she's hearty and joyous or a rose
because she's so loving! These mixed bouquets
come together in the most beautiful arrange-
ments. Just like our friendships, different but
beautifully arranged by the Creator that
we may love, complement, and bless each other.

*Tea
Room*

Dance like no one's watching
Sing like no one's listening
and celebrate . . . every day!

Museum

This is the day the Lord has made;
let us rejoice and be glad in it—Psalm 118:24

 Church *Mountains*

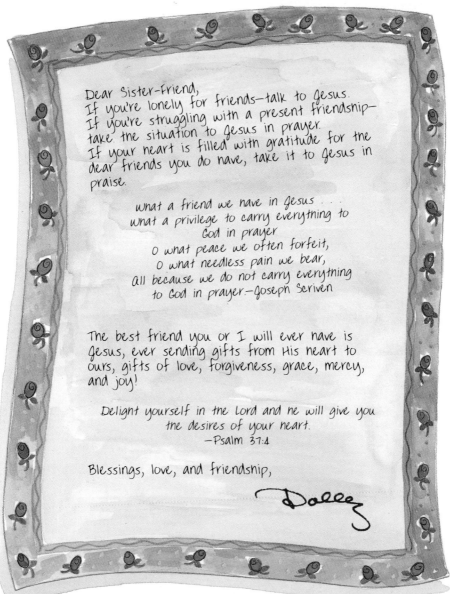

Dear Sister-Friend,
If you're lonely for friends—talk to Jesus.
If you're struggling with a present friendship—
take the situation to Jesus in prayer.
If your heart is filled with gratitude for the
dear friends you do have, take it to Jesus in
praise.

What a friend we have in Jesus . . .
What a privilege to carry everything to
God in prayer
O what peace we often forfeit,
O what needless pain we bear,
All because we do not carry everything
to God in prayer.—Joseph Scriven

The best friend you or I will ever have is
Jesus, ever sending gifts from His heart to
ours, gifts of love, forgiveness, grace, mercy,
and joy!

Delight yourself in the Lord and he will give you
the desires of your heart.
—Psalm 37:4

Blessings, love, and friendship,

Dalee